EYE OPENERS

Dinosaurs

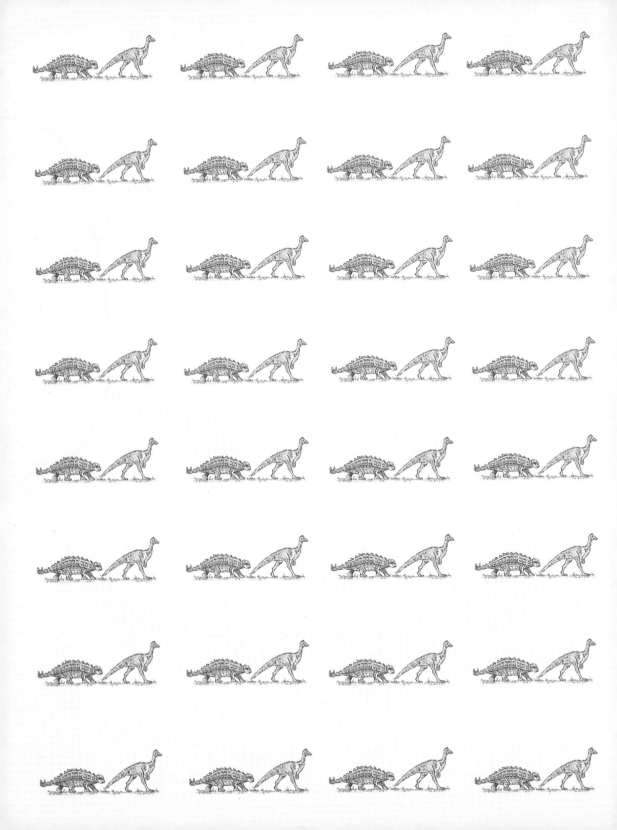

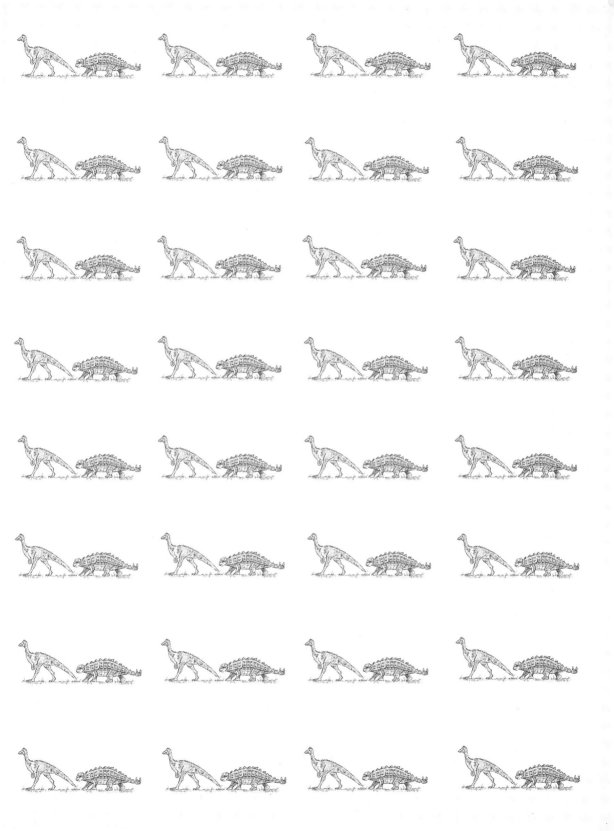

www.dk.com

Senior Editor Jane Yorke   **Senior Art Editor** Mark Richards
Editor Dawn Sirett   **Art Editor** Jane Coney
Designer Karen Fielding   **Production** Marguerite Fenn

Photography by Colin Keates
Illustrations on pages 6-21 by Jane Cradock-Watson and Dave Hopkins
Illustrations on pages 2-3, 22-23, and cover by Martine Blaney
Models supplied by Department of Public Services,
Modelmaking and Taxidermy Section, Natural History Museum, London

Eye Openers ®
First published in Great Britain in 1991
by Dorling Kindersley Limited,
9 Henrietta Street, London WC2E 8PS
Reprinted 1992, 1993

2 4 6 8 10 9 7 5 3

A pronunciation guide to the dinosaur names in this book:

Stegosaurus STEG-oh-SAW-rus	**Tyrannosaurus rex** tie-RAN-oh-SAW-rus REX	**Triceratops** try-SER-a-tops
Hypsilophodon hip-see-LOAF-oh-don	**Diplodocus** dip-LOD-oh-kus	**Deinonychus** dy-NON-ee-kus
Scolosaurus SCOL-oh-SAW-rus	**Gallimimus** GAL-ih-MIME-us	

A CIP catalogue record for this book
is available from the British Library.

ISBN 0-7513-5951-3

Reproduced by Colourscan, Singapore
Printed in China

EYE OPENERS

Dinosaurs

Written by Angela Royston

London • New York • Sydney • Delhi

Stegosaurus

Dinosaurs lived long ago, before there were any people. We know about these giant animals today because their fossilized bones have been found in rocks. Scientists join up the bones like a jigsaw puzzle. These bones belong to a dinosaur called Stegosaurus.

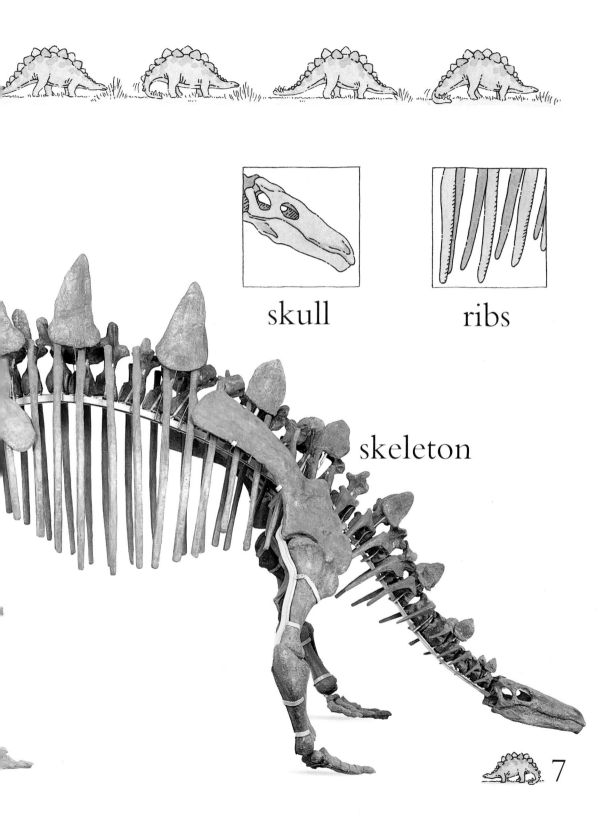

skull

ribs

skeleton

Tyrannosaurus rex

The Tyrannosaurus rex was very fierce. It had a large head, huge jaws, and lots of long, sharp teeth. It hunted dinosaurs and other animals. The Tyrannosaurus rex was longer than a bus. This dinosaur probably moved slowly because it was so big.

tail

head

arm

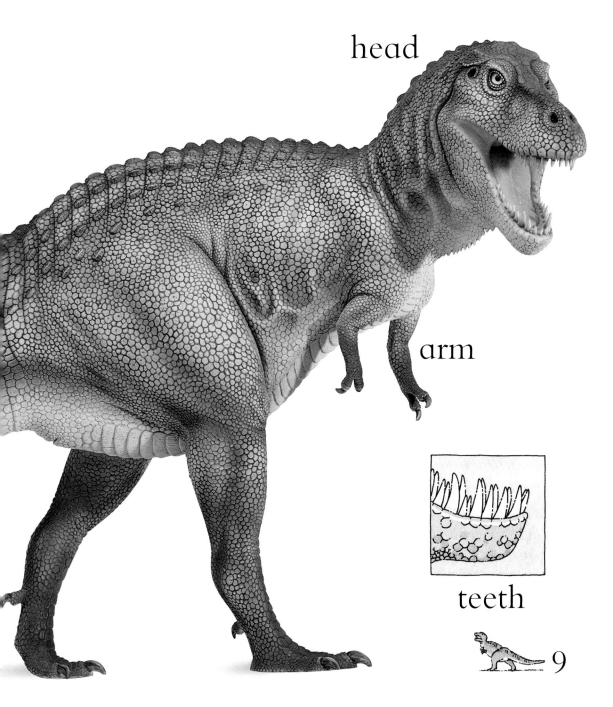

teeth

9

Triceratops

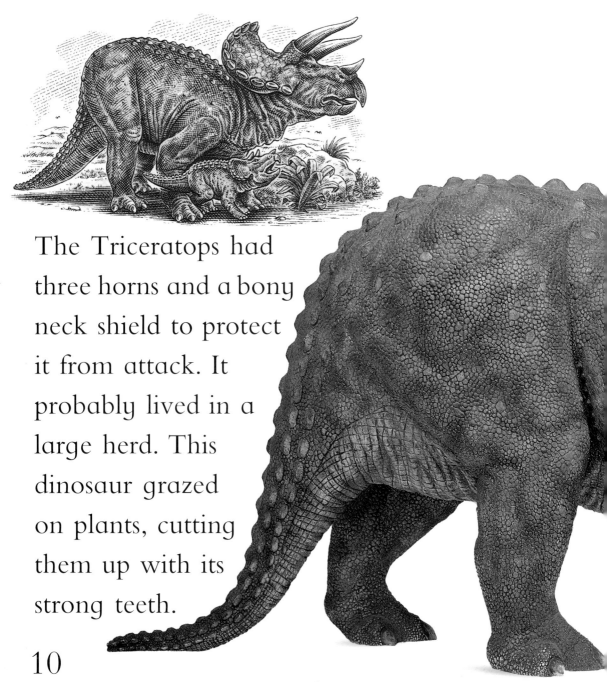

The Triceratops had
three horns and a bony
neck shield to protect
it from attack. It
probably lived in a
large herd. This
dinosaur grazed
on plants, cutting
them up with its
strong teeth.

10

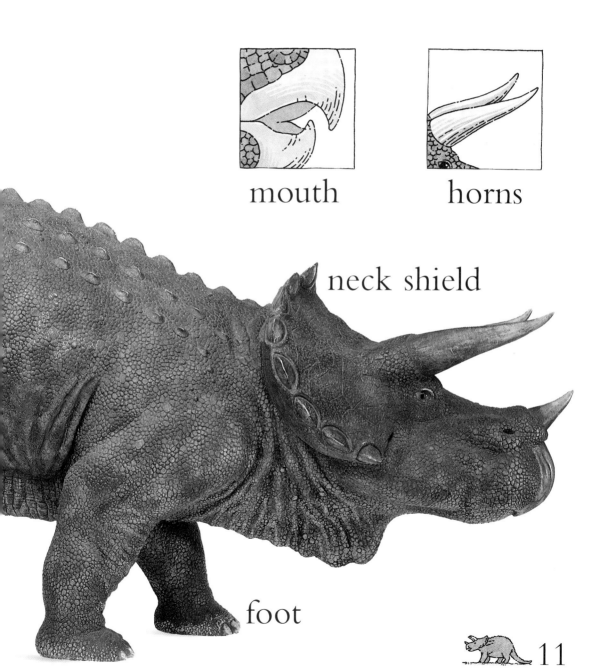

mouth

horns

neck shield

foot

Hypsilophodon

Hypsilophodons were small dinosaurs that ate low-growing plants. They could run fast to escape from danger. Like most dinosaurs, their babies hatched from eggs. Dinosaurs laid their eggs in hollow-shaped nests in the ground.

tail

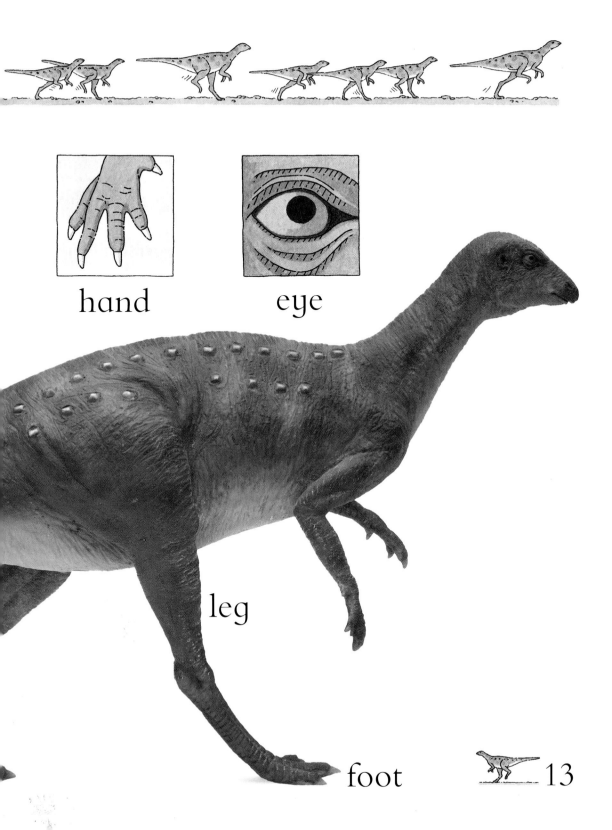

hand

eye

leg

foot

13

Diplodocus

This dinosaur is one of the biggest animals ever to have lived on land. It had a very long neck and an even longer tail. The Diplodocus ate plants. It stood on its back legs to reach leaves high in the tree-tops.

leg

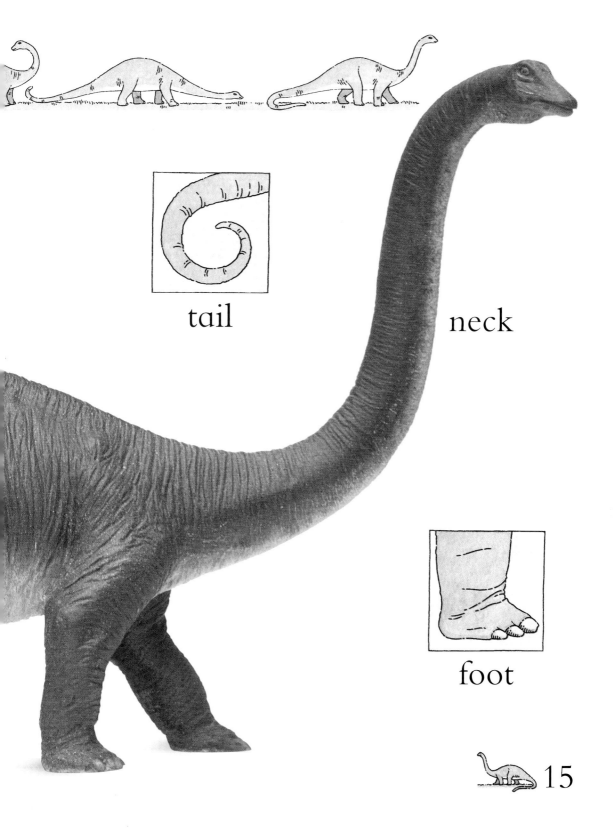

tail

neck

foot

15

Deinonychus

Deinonychus means "terrible claw". This small dinosaur had a huge, curved claw on each foot and three long claws on each hand. The Deinonychus had sharp teeth and ate dinosaurs and other animals. It probably hunted for food in a group.

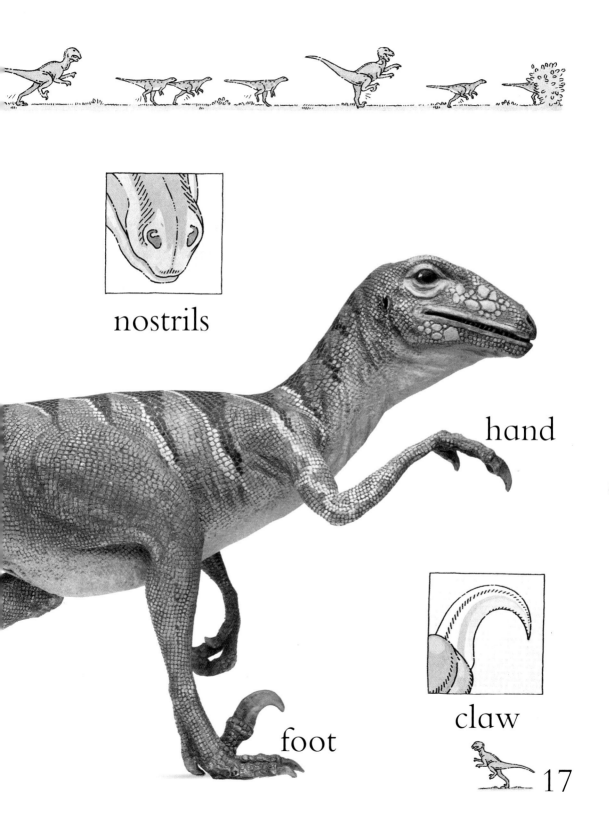

nostrils

hand

foot

claw

17

Scolosaurus

The Scolosaurus was well protected from attack. It was covered in bony armour and had two pointed spikes on the end of its tail. This dinosaur could use its tail to knock over an enemy. The Scolosaurus ate plants.

tail

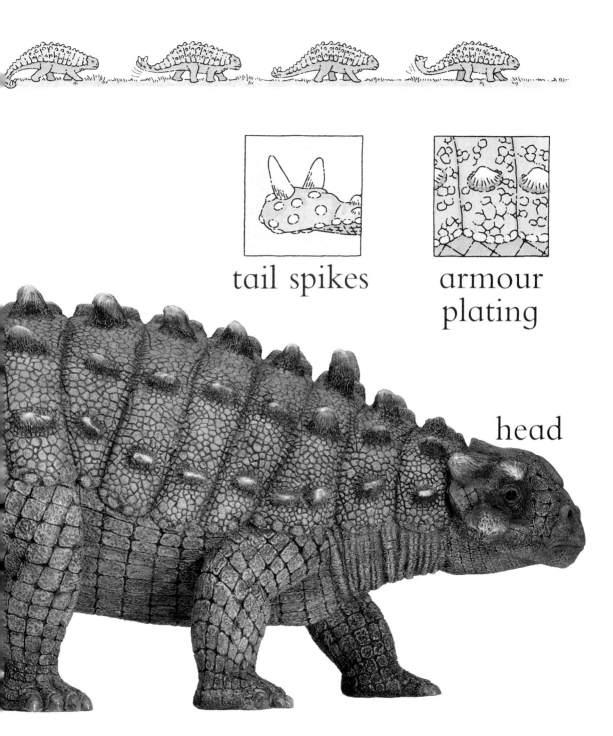

tail spikes

armour
plating

head

19

Gallimimus

The Gallimimus looked like a giant bird. It had a hard beak and no teeth. It might have eaten lizards and insects, plants, or even dinosaur eggs. The Gallimimus had strong back legs and was a fast runner. Like many dinosaurs, its skin was scaly.

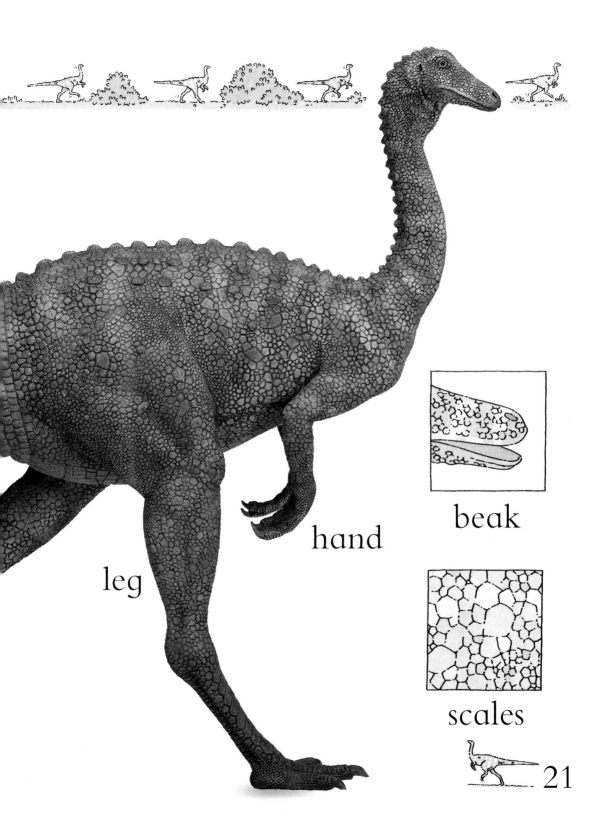

hand

beak

leg

scales

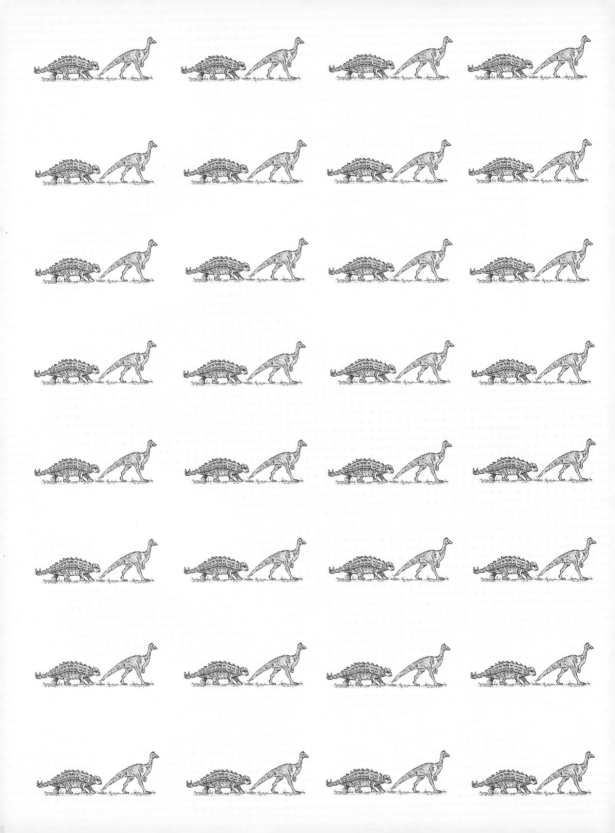

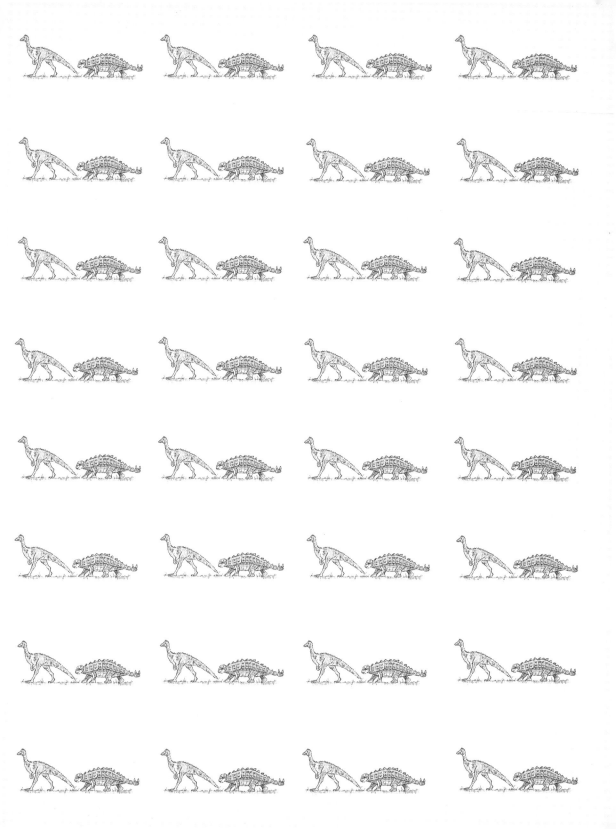